MAKING TRACKS WITH MICHAEL

Bike off into strange and unknown parts. Climb into the sidecar of a BMW and careen around our land with Michael J. Doonesbury, with Mark, a computer drop-out, with Joanie Caucus, a thirty-nine-year-old runaway housewife, and with other transients who believe that America has yet to be definitively discovered.

GARRY TRUDEAU, twenty-six, is a loner. He knows no home, and his only companion is an old collie.

D0980072

Call Me When You Find America

a *Doonesbury* book by G. B. Trudeau

BANTAM BOOKS
TORONTO · NEW YORK · LONDON

CALL ME WHEN YOU FIND AMERICA
*A Bantam Book / published by arrangement with
Holt, Rinehart and Winston*

PRINTING HISTORY
Holt, Rinehart and Winston edition / October 1973
2nd printing ...... March 1974   4th printing ... September 1974
3rd printing .... May 1974   5th printing .... April 1975
Bantam edition / February 1976

*Bantam Books are published by Bantam Books, Inc. Its trade-
mark, consisting of the words "Bantam Books" and the por-
trayal of a bantam, is registered in the United States Patent
Office and in other countries. Marca Registrada. Bantam
Books, Inc., 666 Fifth Avenue, New York, New York 10019.*

PRINTED IN THE UNITED STATES OF AMERICA

0 9 8 7 6 5 4 3 2

GOOD EVENING. THIS IS JOHN CHANCELLOR BRINGING YOU LIVE COVERAGE OF THE PRESIDENT'S TRIP TO WATTS.

THE MEMBERS OF THE PRESS HAVE BEEN VERY ANXIOUSLY AWAITING THE ARRIVAL OF THE PRESIDENT, WHO IS RIGHT NOW HOVERING OVER THE FAMOUS GHETTO IN HIS HELICOPTER.

...NOW THE HELICOPTER IS TOUCHING DOWN... THE ENGINE IS TURNED OFF... THE DOOR OPENS.. MR. NIXON, WAVING TO THE PEOPLE, APPEARS... AND NOW STEPS DOWN INTO ONE OF WATTS' LARGEST USED CAR LOTS..

THE PRESIDENT SEEMS STRANGELY AT HOME.

11

IT IS A SOLEMN MOMENT HERE IN WATTS.

THE PRESIDENT CARRIES A WREATH, A WREATH WHICH HONORS THE MANY BRAVE MEN WHO FOUGHT IN THE WATTS RIOTS OF 1965.

THE PARTY IS NOW APPROACHING THE BURNED-OUT STOREFRONT... THE LOCAL DRUM CORPS PLAYS A ROLL..

.. AND FINALLY,... THE PRESIDENT PLACES THE WREATH ON THE TOMB OF THE UNKNOWN INNOCENT BYSTANDER.

YES. MR. SEMPLE.

MR. PRESIDENT, LAST NIGHT, AFTER YOU PARACHUTED THROUGH THE CAPITOL SKYLIGHTS, YOU MADE AN ADDRESS TO CONGRESS WHICH MANY SENATORS THOUGHT PATRONIZING. ANY COMMENT?

MR. SEMPLE, I AM AWARE OF THIS CRITICISM, AND I FEEL IT UNFAIR. I TRIED TO DESCRIBE MY TRIP TO WATTS WITH CARE AND TACT.

BUT, SIR, DO YOU THINK "A GLORIOUS SAFARI" WAS THE WORDING YOU WERE AFTER?

18

SON, I'VE DECIDED YOU'RE GOING TO HAVE TO PAY YOUR OWN WAY THROUGH COLLEGE NEXT YEAR.

WHY?

AS I POINTED OUT TO YOU OVER SPRING VACATION, I'M SICK OF GETTING NO RETURNS ON MY INVESTMENT IN YOUR EDUCATION!

WHAT YOU GOT IN MIND, DAD?

GOOD REPORT CARDS, FOR EXAMPLE! YOU NEVER BROUGHT ANY OF **THEM** HOME! AND YOU NEVER GOT ELECTED TO ANYTHING! NOT ONCE!

DAD...

AND SPORTS TROPHIES! YOU NEVER BROUGHT HOME *ONE LOUSY SPORTS TROPHY!*

I CAN'T BELIEVE IT! THIS GARAGE IS AN ABSOLUTE HOLE!

I'VE TRIED TO BE FAIR WITH YOU, MARK! I GAVE YOU A DECENT PLACE TO LAY YOUR SLEEPING BAG! BUT YOU TOOK ADVANTAGE OF ME!

DAD.

SORRY, KID, I'VE HAD ENOUGH. FROM NOW ON, CONSIDER YOURSELF COMPLETELY DISOWNED!

DAD...

DAD? DAD WHO?

YOU KNOW, MARCUS, I DON'T THINK WE SHOULD LET THIS HERE SEARCHING FOR AMERICA BUSINESS BECOME THE ONLY IMPETUS FOR OUR JOURNEY!

SURE, SEARCHING FOR AMERICA IS VERY KEY, BUT THERE ARE OTHER DELIGHTS WHICH AWAIT OUR DISCOVERY!

FOR INSTANCE, AS MY GRANDFATHER USED TO SAY TO ME BEFORE OUR FAMILY TRIPS, "CHERCHEZ LES FEMMES!"

WHAT?

KEEP AN EYE PEELED FOR BROADS.

OH.

36

37

WELL, WE'VE GOT TO GET BACK ON THE ROAD, ZONKER.

I SURE HATE TO GO BEFORE ALL THE DELEGATES ACTUALLY LEAVE. SOMETHING IMPORTANT MIGHT HAPPEN AND I'LL MISS IT.

MR. CHAIRMAN, THE DELEGATION FROM RHODE ISLAND REQUESTS PERMISSION TO SEND OUT FOR SOME PIZZA! 4zzz

I'M OFF.

TAKE CARE.

 MAN, THEY WEREN'T KIDDING ABOUT THE SMOG IN LOS ANGELES. IT'S UNBELIEVABLE!

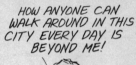 HOW ANYONE CAN WALK AROUND IN THIS CITY EVERY DAY IS BEYOND ME!

 MAN, I CAN'T EVEN SEE THE STREET SIGNS!..

MIKE, THIS IS RIDICULOUS! LOOK, I AGREE..

49

MA'AM, WE'VE COME ALMOST 400 MILES SINCE YOU STOPPED US. BEFORE WE GO ANY FURTHER, MAYBE YOU BETTER TELL US WHO YOU ARE AND WHERE YOU WANT TO GO...

FAIR ENOUGH, BOYS. MY NAME IS JOANIE CAUCUS AND I'M RUNNING AWAY FROM MY HUSBAND CLINTON. IN BRIEF, I GOT FED UP WITH THE MEANINGLESS ROLES THAT DEFINED MY LIFE.

I WANT TO FIND A NEW TOWN WHERE I CAN START A NEW LIFE... A PLACE WHERE I CAN LIVE OUT A GRACEFUL REPRIEVAL, A PLACE WHERE I CAN BEGIN ANEW.

CLEVELAND, SAY.

HMM..

MS. CAUCUS — IF YOU DON'T MIND A PERSONAL QUESTION, WHEN DID YOU FIRST START HAVING DIFFICULTIES WITH YOUR HUSBAND CLINTON?

WELL, MIKE, IT'S DIFFICULT TO PINPOINT IT, BUT I GUESS IT MIGHT HAVE BEEN ONE NIGHT LAST SUMMER, WHEN HIS BOWLING BUDDIES CAME TO DINNER...

AT THE END OF THE MEAL, ONE OF HIS FRIENDS COMPLIMENTED ME ON MY FRENCH FRIES. CLINTON LEANED BACK IN HIS CHAIR, AND SAID WITH A BIG, STUPID GRIN, "MY WIFE, I THINK I'LL KEEP HER!"

I BROKE HIS NOSE.

GOTTA LETTER FROM MIKE HERE, ZONKER...

WELL, FOR LAND SAKE, BOY, READ IT!

"DEAR FRIENDS: BY THE TIME YOU GET THIS, MARK AND I WILL BE IN CHICAGO. WE EXPECT TO MAKE IT BACK TO WALDEN BY EARLY NEXT WEEK.

"WE ARE BRINGING WITH US A BEAUTIFUL, SENSITIVE, BUT CONFUSED LADY NAMED JOANIE, WHOM WE PICKED UP IN DENVER. WE BEFRIENDED HER BECAUSE SHE HAD NO ONE ELSE TO TURN TO DURING A MOMENT OF CRISIS.

"SO IT'S NOT WHAT YOU THINK."

WHEW.

MS. CAUCUS, I STILL DON'T UNDERSTAND WHY YOU LEFT YOUR HUSBAND. DIDN'T YOU HAVE A NICE HOME AND LOVING CHILDREN?..

YES, BOOPSIE, BUT FOR ME, THE ROLE OF LITTLE HOMEMAKER WAS STIFLING. I SUDDENLY BECAME AWARE THAT I WAS DEFINING MYSELF STRICTLY IN TERMS OF OTHERS— MY HUSBAND AND KIDS.

IT BECAME IMPORTANT TO ME TO HAVE SOMETHING OF MY OWN, TO BE INVOLVED IN A PERSONAL PASSION..

OH, YES, I KNOW HOW IMPORTANT THAT IS..

I MYSELF AM ACTIVE IN THE AREA OF CHEERLEADING.

YOU'RE PROBABLY ALL WONDERING WHY I'VE ASKED YOU HERE..

YES..

YEAH.

RIGHT.

YES, I KNOW I AM...

AS YOU KNOW, MS. CAUCUS HAS BEEN STAYING WITH US WHILE SEARCHING FOR A JOB. WELL, I'VE BEEN THINKING THAT WE SHOULD MAKE THE ARRANGEMENT PERMANENT!! ALL IN FAVOR, SAY "RIGHT ON."

RIGHT ON!!

THE RIGHT ONS HATH IT!

YEA!!

CLAP!
CLAP!
CLAP!
CLAP!
CLAP!
CLAP!
CLAP!

GIRLS, I'D LIKE TO TALK TO YOU ABOUT GROWING UP TO BE MOMMIES.

GROWING UP TO BE A MOMMY IS ONE OF THE MOST WONDERFUL THINGS A LITTLE GIRL CAN WANT TO DO. *BUT*... THERE ARE OTHER THINGS IN LIFE SHE CAN DO AS WELL...

FOR INSTANCE, SHE CAN WORK HER HEAD OFF AND SHOW ALL THOSE ARROGANT BOYS THAT SHE'S JUST AS CAPABLE AND *INTELLIGENT* AND *CREATIVE* AS ANY *LITTLE STUD AROUND!*

YOU'RE A "LIBBIE," AREN'T YOU, MS. CAUCUS?

YOU BET, HONEY.

HAVE YOU BEEN DOWN TO VISIT JOANIE AT THE DAY CARE CENTER YET?

NO... HOW'S HER NEW JOB COMING?

OKAY, I GUESS... SHE'S BEEN ADMINISTERING CONSCIOUSNESS RAISING SESSIONS TO THE GIRLS...

TERRIFIC!

I DUNNO.. JOANIE MAY BE ASKING TOO MUCH OF LITTLE GIRLS OF THAT AGE..

NONSENSE! I'M SURE SHE'S HANDLING IT BEAUTIFULLY.

WAAH! I DON'T WANNA BE A BUILDING CONTRACTOR!

NOW DEAR...

HEY, CHIEF, I FINISHED THAT PROFILE ON B.D. AND HIS RETURN TO FOOTBALL.

GOOD WORK, ZONKER HARRIS, ACE REPORTER!

"B.D., THE GREAT GRIDIRON FIELD MARSHAL, LEANED BACK IN HIS CHAIR AND DRAINED HIS BEER CAN BEFORE CRUSHING IT IN ONE MIGHTY PAW."

"'TELL ME, B.D.,' I ASKED, 'WHAT IS IT ABOUT FOOT-BALL THAT YOU LOVE SO MUCH THAT YOU WOULD RETURN TO THE GRUELING ROUTINES AND HOURS OF FATIGUING DRILLS AND PRACTICES?'

"'I LOVE BREAKING HEADS,' REPLIED THE ALLEGED HUMAN BEING."

'BYE, MOM! BE GOOD NOW!

SHE'S A COURAGEOUS SOUL, PHRED.

SHE CERTAINLY IS. SHE'S PUT IN THOUSANDS OF MILES ON THE ROAD OVER THE YEARS.

AND FOR A REFUGEE, SHE'S PRETTY RESOURCE-FUL. SEE THAT KNAPSACK SHE'S GOT ON? SHE GOT THAT FROM AN ABANDONED FIREBASE.

WHERE'D SHE GET THE MOTORCYCLE?

I'M NOT SURE.

GOOD MORNING, DAD.

WAS THAT REMARK REALLY NECESSARY?

SORRY.